WORKBO

AQA GCSE (9–1)

Citizenship

- Full topic coverage
- Over 270 questions
- Answers free online

Mike Mitchell

HODDER
EDUCATION
AN HACHETTE UK COMPANY

The Publishers would like to thank the following for permission to reproduce copyright material.

Photo credits

p.85 *t* © FETHI NASRI/AFP/Getty Images; **p.88** © Shutterstock; **p.94** © Sander Chamid/SCS/ AFLO/Alamy Live News; **p.96** © Alexey Fedorenko - stock.adobe.com.

Acknowledgements

p.41 From The Universal Declaration of Human Rights © 2015 United Nations. Reprinted with the permission of the United Nations.

Orders: please contact Hachette UK Distribution, Hely Hutchinson Centre, Milton Road, Didcot, Oxfordshire, OX11 7HH. Telephone: +44 (0)1235 827827. Email education@hachette. co.uk Lines are open from 9 a.m. to 5 p.m., Monday to Friday. You can also order through our website: www.hoddereducation.co.uk

ISBN: 978 1 3983 1720 8

© Mike Mitchell 2021

First published in 2021 by

Hodder Education,

An Hachette UK Company

Carmelite House

50 Victoria Embankment

London EC4Y 0DZ

www.hoddereducation.co.uk

Impression number   10 9 8 7 6 5 4 3 2

Year   2025 2024 2023 2022

Cover photo © Jacob Lund - stock.adobe.com

Illustrations by Integra Software Services Pvt. Ltd., Pondicherry, India

Typeset by Integra Software Services Pvt. Ltd., Pondicherry, India

Printed in India

A catalogue record for this title is available from the British Library.

Contents

About this book

1   This workbook will help you to prepare for AQA GCSE Citizenship Studies (9–1).

2   AQA GCSE Citizenship Studies (9–1) is assessed by:
- **Paper 1: Active citizenship and Politics and participation**
  Paper 1 lasts for 1 hour and 45 minutes and is worth 50 per cent of the GCSE. The paper has a mixture of multiple-choice, short-answer, source-based and extended-answer questions totalling 80 marks.
- **Paper 2: Life in modern Britain and Rights and responsibilities**
  Paper 2 lasts for 1 hour and 45 minutes and is worth 50 per cent of the GCSE. The paper has a mixture of multiple-choice, short-answer, source-based and extended-answer questions totalling 80 marks.

There are no optional questions on the exam papers so candidates should attempt to answer all the questions.

3   For each topic in this workbook there are:
- practice questions for each sub-topic of the specification
- spaces for you to write or plan your answers
- exam-style questions to help you practise and prepare for your exams.

4   **Answering the questions** will help you to build your skills and meet the assessment objectives AO1 (knowledge and understanding), AO2 (application) and AO3 (analysis and evaluation).

5   **Example student answers** are included throughout the questions to help you understand how to gain the most marks.

6   Icons next to the question will help you to identify:

     where your calculations skills are tested

     where questions draw on synoptic knowledge, i.e. content from more than one topic.

7   **You still need** to read your textbook and refer to your revision guides and lesson notes.

8   **Marks available** are indicated for all questions so that you can gauge the level of detail required in your answers.

9   Answers are available at: www.hoddereducation.co.uk/workbookanswers

Theme 1 Life in modern Britain

This theme covers what it means to be a British citizen in today's society, the values that underpin our society, how our identities are formed and what they comprise. It also looks at the role of the traditional and new media, as well as Britain's role and impact in international organisations and events. The Active Citizenship element of this theme is covered in Theme 4.

What are the principles and values that underpin British society?

Practice questions ?

Principles and values in British society today

1   Identify **one** of the fundamental principles of British life as identified by the UK government. (AO1)

1 mark

....

....

Source A: Russia and human rights

Russia is subject to rulings by the European Court of Human Rights. In June 2007, 22.5 per cent of all the courts' pending cases were being brought by Russian citizens against their own government. The violations of human rights included torture of people by the police, security forces and prison guards; cruelty in orphanages; racism and murder of people from minority ethnic groups.

2   Discuss **two** reasons why such cases are unlikely to be brought to the European Court of Human Rights by UK citizens about the British government. (AO2)

4 marks

1 ....

....

....

....

....

2 ....

....

....

....

....

3 Considering a range of views, to what extent is total individual liberty achievable in modern Britain? (AO3)   8 marks

....

....

....

....

....

....

....

....

....

....

Rights, duties and freedoms of citizens

4 Define what is meant by a 'duty'. (AO1)   1 mark

....

....

Source B: Civil liberties in the USA

The US government is obliged by many constitutional provisions to respect the individual citizen's basic rights. Some civil liberties were specified in the original eighteenth-century written constitution. The Bill of Rights of 1791 added further rights such as in regard to religious freedom, and the right of peaceful assembly and petition. Another right is the right to keep and bear arms.

5 Compare **two** ways in which the situation in the USA regarding rights and how they are determined, as outlined in **Source B**, differs from that in the UK. (AO2)   4 marks

Example student answer

1   In the UK, citizens are not allowed to keep or bear arms.

2   In the UK, rights are not set out in a single document. The UK does not have a written constitution.

AO2: The first response identifies a right that does not exist in the UK: the ability to bear arms (weapons). The second response clearly identifies that the UK does not have a written constitution, so laws are easily changed by Parliament. This indicates knowledge of how rights are determined. Awarded 4 marks.

6 Rights within a society can change and develop over time.

Considering a range of examples, examine why these changes have taken place. (AO3)

8 marks

....

....

....

....

....

....

....

....

....

....

....

Identities

7 Using an example, explain what is meant by 'group identity'. (AO1)

2 marks

....

....

....

....

Source C: The concept of European identity

The idea of a European identity involves geographic, historic and cultural factors. These factors all contribute to the idea of a European identity, but without cancelling out ideas of individual national identity.

The European Union, by establishing rights for every citizen of the Union through the Charter of Fundamental Rights, has created a legal status of citizens of the European Union.

8   Discuss **two** reasons why national identity appears to be more strongly rooted than European identity. (AO2)   **4 marks**

1   ....

    ....

    ....

2   ....

    ....

    ....

9   'Increasingly many people see themselves as global citizens.'

    Considering a range of views, to what extent do you agree or disagree with this statement? (AO3)   **8 marks**

....

....

....

....

....

....

....

....

....

....

....

....

What do we mean by identity?

The UK and identity

10 England is the dominant part of the UK by population. What approximate percentage of the UK population lives in England? (AO1)

Shade in the **one** correct answer.

1 mark

A   55%

B   60%

C   75%

D   85%

E   90%

Source A: National identity

> The 2012 census asked people in the various nations of the United Kingdom how they would describe their national identity:
>
> **England:** 69.5% English; 31.4% British
>
> **Scotland:** 82.7% Scottish; 26.7% British
>
> **Wales:** 64.6% Welsh; 26.7% British; 12.8% English
>
> **Northern Ireland:** 48.4% British; 29.4% Northern Irish; 28.4% Irish

11 Considering the data in **Source A**, identify **two** conclusions that arise about how the nations of the UK feel about identifying themselves as British. (AO2)

4 marks

1 ....

....

....

....

....

2 ....

....

....

....

....

12 'There is no such thing as a British identity.'

Considering a range of views, to what extent do you agree or disagree with the statement? (AO3)　　　　8 marks

....

....

....

....

....

....

....

....

....

....

....

The UK's changing population

13 What is the difference between net migration and emigration? (AO1)　　　　2 marks

....

....

....

....

Source B: Impact of migration on UK cities

Data indicates that new immigrants move to cities that are economically successful.

Evidence indicates that these new migrants have a positive impact on wages, productivity and employment of local people. Their skills tend to complement the local work force which leads to greater innovation and increased productivity. Evidence also indicates that they are more likely to be self-employed and innovators.

14 Consider **two** reasons other than those mentioned in **Source B** why a government may wish to encourage immigration to the UK. (AO2)　　　　4 marks

Reason 1: ....

....

....

....

Reason 2: ....

....

....

....

15 'The UK should open its door to any person to come and settle in the United Kingdom.'
Considering a range of views, what are the implications of such a policy? (AO3)   **8 marks**

Example student answer

Many people think that we should allow anyone who wants to come and live in the UK to do so. They believe that there is evidence to show that migrants are a boost to the economy and have helped develop many new businesses. Living in a multicultural society has benefited the UK which is seen as a cultural hub. Many migrants who come to the UK wish to improve their lives and are escaping persecution or deprivation in their own countries or are caught in the middle of civil wars. So many would argue we have a humanitarian responsibility to those in need.

Those who oppose what they call an open-door policy, state that it becomes difficult to control the numbers of migrants and that large numbers of migrants place a burden on already overstretched public services and housing.

The overall evidence is that migration benefits the UK economically and that many who come actually work in the public services. Over recent years the number of migrants settling in the UK has increased greatly, many coming from EU countries. While some return to their native countries, especially those who come here to study, most settle in the UK. Clearly, if large numbers arrive in the UK year after year, the government would have to put plans in place to assist communities regarding growth in population, housing and public service needs.

AO3: This response covers a range of points both for and against an open-door policy. The response draws together the main issues in some concluding comments. A range of views are covered and various implications are considered. Both elements of the questions are covered. Awarded 8 marks.

Values in a democratic and diverse society

16 The UK is a multicultural society. Using an example, define what is meant by this phrase. (AO1)   **2 marks**

....

....

....

....

Source C: Multiculturalism

> The concept of multiculturalism has underpinned post-war British society. In other countries, such as France, they place an emphasis on a policy of assimilation into French culture and life.

17 Describe **one** benefit and **one** disadvantage regarding the emphasis on multiculturalism in the UK. (AO2)　　　　　**4 marks**

Benefit: ....

....

....

....

Disadvantage: ....

....

....

....

18 Evaluate the actions that a local community could undertake to help develop mutual respect and understanding in a locally diverse society. (AO3)　　　**8 marks**

....

....

....

....

....

....

....

....

....

....

....

....

Identity and multiple identities

19 Using an example, define what is meant when a person is described as having multiple identities. (AO1)　　　　　**2 marks**

....

....

....

....

Source D: Identity

Individuals acquire their identity in many ways. A range of factors influence the nature of a person's identity. Gender, age and sexual orientation are three such factors.

20 Describe **two** factors other than those listed that influence an individual's identity. (AO2)   **4 marks**

1 ....

....

....

....

2 ....

....

....

....

21 Examine the reasons why some areas of the United Kingdom have a more ethnically diverse population than others. (AO3)   **8 marks**

....

....

....

....

....

....

....

....

....

....

What is the role of the media and the free press?

The rights, responsibilities and role of the media

22 Define what is meant by 'freedom of the press'. (AO1)   1 mark

....

....

Source A: Role of the media

> Both the press and television in the United Kingdom are regulated and citizens can hold them to account for what they print and broadcast. Internet and social media companies argue they should be treated differently from other media formats.

23 Discuss **two** arguments that the social media companies put forward to
support their point of view. (AO2)   4 marks

1 ....

....

....

....

2 ....

....

....

....

24 Using case studies, assess the influence of the media in holding those in
power to account. (AO3)   8 marks

....

....

....

....

....

....

....

....

....

....

The right of the media to investigate and report

25 Identify **one** action a person can take if they believe the press has published an inaccurate story about them. (AO1)

1 mark

....

....

26 The media in the UK often campaign on issues to draw them to the public's attention and also to promote changes in public policy.

Discuss briefly **two** recent successful media campaigns. (AO2)

4 marks

1 ....

....

....

....

2 ....

....

....

27 Examine how the Freedom of Information Act assists the media to carry out investigative journalism. (AO3)

8 marks

....

....

....

....

....

....

....

....

....

....

Press regulation and censorship

28 What is the function of the organisation IMPRESS? (AO1)

1 mark

....

....

Source B: Chinese censorship

Changes in laws regarding national security in Hong Kong mean that there is a legal requirement on social media companies to provide information on their users to the government. If they fail to do so, they face fines and possible imprisonment. As a result of these changes, a number of international social media companies have withdrawn their services from Hong Kong.

29 Compare **two** ways in which the situation described in **Source B** differs from media regulation in the UK. (AO2)   4 marks

1 ....

....

....

....

2 ....

....

....

....

30 'The press should be regulated by the government.'

Considering a range of points of view, to what extent do you agree or disagree with the statement? (AO3)   8 marks

....

....

....

....

....

....

....

....

....

....

....

What is the UK's role in key international organisations?

The role of the UK within key international organisations

31 Which of the following is a military alliance? (AO1)

Shade in the **one** correct answer.

1 mark

A   UN   ◯

B   Council of Europe   ◯

C   The Commonwealth   ◯

D   NATO   ◯

E   WTO   ◯

Source A: The United Nations

In 2020, the UN has 194 members countries and is involved in peacekeeping throughout the world, as well as being involved through its agencies in helping those most in need. The United Kingdom plays a very active role in the work of the United Nations.

32 Consider **two** reasons why the United Kingdom is seen by other countries as one of the most important members of the UN. (AO2)   **4 marks**

1 ....

....

....

2 ....

....

....

33 Assess the benefits to UK citizens of the UK being a signatory of the European Convention on Human Rights. (AO3)   **8 marks**

....

....

....

....

....

....

....

....

....

The UK and the EU

34 The United Kingdom has held two nationwide referendums about its membership of the European Union. The most recent was in 2016. When was the first referendum held? (AO1)

1 mark

A 1970 ⬭

B 1975 ⬭

C 1987 ⬭

D 1997 ⬭

Source B: The 2016 European Union membership referendum

Nation	% vote to leave	% vote to remain	% turnout
England	53.4	46.6	73.0
Scotland	38.0	62.0	67.2
Wales	52.5	47.5	71.7
Northern Ireland	44.2	55.8	62.9

35 Consider **two** reasons why the referendum result in 2016 was seen as a final decision about the UK's membership of the European Union. (AO2)

4 marks

1 ....

....

....

2 ....

....

....

36 'The UK is no longer a member of the EU.'

Considering a range of views, critically assess the claims made about the benefits for the UK of leaving the EU. (AO3)

8 marks

....

....

....

....

....

....

....

....

....

International disputes and conflicts

37 Using an example, explain what is meant by the term 'sanctions'. (AO1)

....

....

....

....

Source C: Military intervention v sanctions

In recent years, UK armed forces have been involved with forces from other countries in military action in such places as Libya, Afghanistan, Iraq and Sierra Leone. The UK government also has a policy of using sanctions to bring about change.

38 Consider **one** advantage of using military action and **one** advantage of the
use of sanctions to resolve an international dispute. (AO2)   4 marks

Military action: ....

....

....

Sanctions: ....

....

....

39 'The UK, since the year 2000, has been involved with other countries in several military
interventions in foreign countries.'

Considering a range of points of view, to what extent has this military intervention
been successful? (AO3)   8 marks

....

....

....

....

....

....

....

....

....

....

....

How non-governmental organisations (NGOs) respond to humanitarian crises

40 Which government department is responsible for UK foreign aid and assistance? (AO1)   1 mark

....

....

Source D: Disaster assistance

Often when there is a natural disaster, advertisements sponsored by the Disasters Emergency Committee will appear, requesting public donations of money. This umbrella group provides funding for a range of NGOs and leading UK charities. In addition, the UK government was the first country in the G7 to honour the UK target set in 1970, to ring-fence 0.7 per cent of Gross National Income for international aid.

41 Discuss **two** reasons why the UK government prefers to work with NGOs rather than providing direct aid to the countries needing help. (AO2)   4 marks

1 ....

....

....

....

2 ....

....

....

....

42 Using case studies, examine the role and success of NGOs in regard to humanitarian crises.   8 marks

....

....

....

....

....

....

....

....

....

....

Synoptic question

The last 8-mark question at the end of each of the three themes is a synoptic question. This question aims to draw upon your knowledge and understanding across different parts of the specification.

43 Discrimination still exists in modern Britain. To what extent has the introduction of anti-discrimination laws since 1960 improved the situation?

In your answer you should consider:

*   a range of forms of discrimination
*   the effectiveness of anti-discrimination legislation. (AO3)   8 marks

....

....

....

....

....

....

....

....

....

....

....

Paper 2, Section A: Life in modern Britain

1 Which of the following bodies is responsible in the UK for the regulation of the television industry? 1 mark

Shade in the **one** correct answer.

A   OFQUAL ⬭

B   IMPRESS ⬭

C   OFWAT ⬭

D   OFCOM ⬭

2 Using **one** example, explain the term 'censorship'. 2 marks

....

....

Source A: President Trump signs order to change internet rules

In the USA, Section 230 of the 1996 Communications Decency Act protects social media companies, such as Facebook and Twitter, from legal liability regarding the content their users post on their sites. Many see the existing law as a fundamental right and protection. President Trump has signed an Executive order removing some of these protections. The companies are challenging the order through the courts.

3 Referring to **Source A**, identify **one** reason for and **one** against making social media companies legally liable for the content on their sites. 4 marks

Reason for: ....

....

....

Reason against: ....

....

....

4 Using an example, define what is meant by 'national identity'. 1 mark

....

....

5 Explain what is meant by the term 'UK net migration'. 2 marks

....

....

....

....

Source B: British or national identity

Most people living in Britain, when asked, say they identify equally with being British or their national identity (Scottish/Welsh/Irish).

- 46 per cent feel British rather than associating with a nation.
- 37 per cent associate with a nation rather than being British.

There are regional and cultural differences.

- In London, Britishness is more evident.
- Those from a BAME background are more likely to identify as British than Scottish, Welsh or English.

6   Referring to **Source B**, consider why London and those from a BAME background are more likely to identify as British rather than associating with one of the UK nations.   4 marks

London: ....

....

....

....

BAME: ....

....

....

....

7   Name **one** non-European country that is a member of NATO.   1 mark

....

8   Name the body that was responsible for drafting the European Convention of Human Rights.   1 mark

....

9   Identify the **two** cities where the Parliament of the European Union meets. Shade in the **two** correct answers.   2 marks

A   Paris   ⬭

B   London   ⬭

C   Berlin   ⬭

D   Brussels   ⬭

E   Frankfurt   ⬭

F   Strasbourg   ⬭

G   Madrid   ⬭

Source C: The Commonwealth

The Commonwealth is a voluntary association of independent countries, most of which were former colonies of the British Empire. Its members represent about one third of the entire world population. It has a charter setting out its values and all members must support the charter. The Head of the Commonwealth is Queen Elizabeth II. Heads of government of the member states meet every two years at a conference. It has a small number of administrative staff who are based in London. From time to time, member countries have been expelled from the Commonwealth and have to re-apply.

10   Compare the structure and workings of the Commonwealth, as outlined in **Source C**, with the way the European Union functions.

4 marks

....

....

....

....

....

....

11   Define what is meant by the term 'referendum'.

1 mark

....

....

12   The UK is no longer a member of the European Union.

Considering a range of views, examine why some people believe this will benefit the United Kingdom.

8 marks

....

....

....

....

....

....

....

....

....

....

....

13 Using an example, define the term 'NGO'.   **2 marks**

....

....

....

14 The UK government is one of a few that donate 0.7 per cent of GDP to international aid, roughly £15 billion in 2020. Some politicians claim that charity should begin at home, and that these funds should be used to support public services in the UK or to cut taxes.

Considering a range of views, to what extent do you agree or disagree about the level of the UK's international aid spending?

In your answer you should consider:

● the role of international aid
● the nature of the UK budget and spending.   **8 marks**

....

....

....

....

....

....

....

....

....

....

....

....

Theme 2 Rights and responsibilities

This theme covers the nature of laws and the principles upon which they are based, the operation of the justice system and individuals' rights and responsibilities within it. The ways in which the law changes are dealt with as well as the nature of criminality and how criminals are treated. Finally, international agreements in relation to human rights are explored. The Active Citizenship element of this theme is covered in Theme 4.

What laws does a society require and why?

The fundamental principles of law

1 Explain what is meant by the phrase 'equality before the law'. (AO1)   1 mark

....

....

Source A: Trial by jury

In many countries and in some courts in the UK, the decision about guilt or innocence as well as any sentence are decided by a judge or a group of judges. Many people are calling for the end of trials by jury as they believe there are many problems associated with jury trials.

2 Consider **one** advantage and **one** disadvantage of trial by jury. (AO2)   4 marks

Advantage: ....

....

....

Disadvantage: ....

....

....

3 Examine why the 'presumption of innocence' is such an important legal concept. (AO3)   8 marks

....

....

....

....

....

....

....

....

....

....

....

Rules and laws

4   Identify an example of an area of life where rules apply and another area of life
     where laws apply. (AO1)   2 marks

     Rules: ....

....

....

     Laws: ....

....

....

Source B: Justice and fairness

Justice and fairness are central to the way our society operates. While justice relates to how society reacts to events and deals with them, the concept of fairness relates to how citizens are treated by the system: equally and according to the circumstances of an event.

5   Discuss what the implications for a society are when large numbers of its citizens
     do not believe that their society operates based upon the principles of justice
     and fairness. (AO2)   4 marks

....

....

....

....

....

....

6   Examine, using examples, the success of the UK in overcoming discrimination in
     any **two** areas of life by the introduction of laws. (AO3)   8 marks

....

....

....

....

....
....
....
....
....
....

Rights in local to global situations

Source C: Rights and responsibilities

Brett and Naghemeh King were held in prison in Madrid during the summer of 2014, after removing their son Ashya from Southampton General Hospital against medical advice. They were arrested in Madrid and held in prison for 24 hours before extradition proceedings were abandoned. They took Ashya to Prague to have treatment for his cancer that was unavailable in the UK.

7 Discuss how this is a good example of a clash between rights and responsibilities. (AO2)

4 marks

....
....
....
....
....

8 Justify why a government in a crisis situation should have the powers to curtail the rights and freedoms of its citizens. (AO3)

8 marks

....
....
....
....
....
....
....
....
....

What are a citizen's rights and responsibilities within the legal system?

The operation of the justice system

Source A: Police powers of arrest

> One of the most important powers the police have is that of arrest. The police have the power to arrest anywhere and at any time, including on the street, at home or at a workplace.

9   Discuss **two** complaints that are made about some police officers' use of the power of arrest. (AO2)   **4 marks**

1   ....

....

....

....

2   ....

....

....

....

10 Analyse the case made for the UK having a number of regional police forces rather than one national police force. (AO3)   **8 marks**

....

....

....

....

....

....

....

....

....

....

....

....

11 Identify in which court citizens decide if a person is guilty or innocent, and determine the sentence if guilty. (AO1)   **1 mark**

....

Source B: The role and power of judges

> Judges are required to interpret laws in line with the intention of Parliament. Judges are influential in the way they interpret and apply the law, but they may not challenge the validity of an Act of Parliament. They can state that a law is incompatible with the European Convention of Human Rights, but may not dismiss the law for this reason. Senior judges have suggested that there may be limits to Parliament's sovereignty. The Supreme Court ruled against the government regarding Brexit decisions in actions brought by UK citizens.

12 Discuss if the judiciary in the UK should have the power to limit the sovereignty of Parliament. (AO2)   **4 marks**

Example student answer

In the UK, the judiciary is independent from the political system. There is now a Supreme Court in the UK, which was given the power to make judgements about the legality of legislation. The judiciary should have this power, as once elected the government of the UK is largely unaccountable to the people, especially if it has a large majority. In the past, the UK system of government has been called an 'elected dictatorship'.

AO2: The response indicates good knowledge of the operation of the judiciary, especially the Supreme Court. There is clear understanding of the ways in which Parliament granted the courts these powers. Awarded 4 marks.

13 Evaluate why it is important that judges are not political appointees and are independent of government. (AO3)   **8 marks**

....

....

....

....

....

....

....

....

....

....

....

....

14 Identify what is meant by the initials QC after a person's name. (AO1)   1 mark

....

Source C: A case study

A friend calls around to see you and asks your advice regarding their housing problems.

They have just recently moved into rented accommodation but after three weeks they still have not received from the landlord a signed copy of the tenancy agreement or a receipt for their payment into the deposit scheme. They have tried contacting the landlord without success as they are concerned about a gas boiler in the property and have not been given a gas safety certificate.

15 Discuss what the options are regarding seeking help to resolve their problem.
Give a reason for your choice. (AO2)   4 marks

....

....

....

....

....

16 Examine the differing roles of solicitors and barristers within the legal system. (AO3)   8 marks

....

....

....

....

....

....

....

....

....

....

....

Source D: The court structure in England and Wales

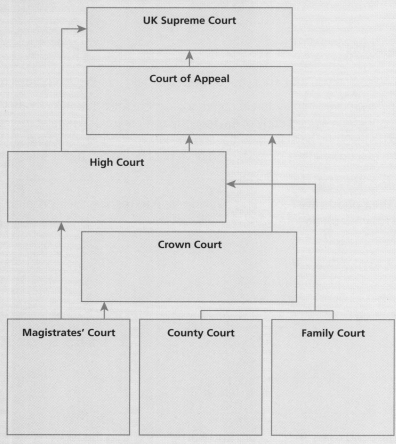

17 The above chart indicates the various courts that form the civil and criminal court structure in England and Wales. Referring to **Source D**, describe the route through the court system of someone charged with a serious criminal offence, who after being found guilty in a lower court, appeals against their conviction. (AO2)   **4 marks**

....

....

....

....

....

....

18 Analyse the case made by those who wish to retain trial by jury. (AO3)   **8 marks**

....

....

....

....

....

....

....

....

....

19 Identify what is meant by the initials ADR. (AO1)   1 mark

....

20 Examine how effective tribunals are in securing citizens' rights. (AO3)   8 marks

....

....

....

....

....

....

....

....

....

....

Rights and legal entitlements of citizens at differing ages

Source E: Rights at different ages

	End of compulsory education	Admission to employment	Minimum age for marriage	Criminal responsibility
UK (2020)	18	18 (can undertake training or apprenticeship at 16)	16 (with parents' permission)	8 (in Scotland) 10 (in England and Wales)
Serbia (2008)	14	15	16	14

21 According to **Source E**, different countries have different ages relating to rights and responsibilities. Discuss **two** reasons why the age to acquire rights varies from one country to another. (AO2)   4 marks

1 ....

....

....

2 ....

....

....

22 Make a case to justify altering all age-related rights or responsibility to a limited number of ages instead of the wide range that exists today. (AO3)   8 marks

....

....

....

....

....

....

....

....

....

How civil law differs from criminal law

23 Name the court system that awards 'damages' as an outcome of a case. (AO1)   1 mark

....

24 Evaluate the argument that for most civil disputes, the legal system does not allow the poorest in society access to justice. (AO3)   8 marks

Example student answer

In the UK there are two types of court cases: criminal and civil. In a criminal case the government meets the legal costs of the defence if the accused cannot. In civil cases the dispute is between individuals or against official bodies. In the case of government agencies there is some free legal support paid for by the government, but where it is a dispute between individuals, for example libel or divorce cases, there is no government support.

If you are poor you either have to borrow funds, crowd fund, or defend yourself in court. Lawyers do offer no win no fee support, but this doesn't apply to all cases. Therefore if you are poor your access to the court system is limited. Also, those with funds can use the law to delay issues, demand further information and cause the other person either to take on more debt or just to give up contesting their case.

AO3: The response indicates a knowledge of a legal system and makes a clear distinction between civil and criminal law. Several valid points are discussed. Awarded 8 marks.

How the legal systems differ within the UK

Source F: The court structure in Scotland

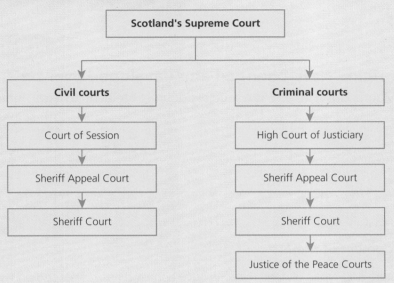

25 Describe **two** ways in which the Scottish court system differs from that in England. (AO2)   **4 marks**

1 ....

....

....

2 ....

....

....

26 Examine why different parts of the UK have different legal systems. (AO3)   **8 marks**

....

....

....

....

....

....

....

....

....

....

How has the law developed over time, and how does the law protect the citizen and deal with criminals?

How citizens' rights have changed and developed over time

27 Explain why Magna Carta in 1215 is a crucial document relating to legal rights. (AO1) **2 marks**

....

....

....

....

Source A: Development of rights

> Over time, the nature and types of rights citizens have acquired has developed and changed. It can be said that the development of rights has gone through stages:
> - Legal rights
> - Political rights
> - Religious rights
> - Economic rights
> - Welfare rights
> - Personal rights

28 Discuss the nature of any of the rights citizens of the UK have acquired, related to any **two** of the above suggested stages. (AO2)   **4 marks**

1 Stage: .... Right: ....

....

....

....

2 Stage: .... Right: ....

....

....

....

Common law and legislation

Source B: Common law and Brexit

In 2016, Gina Miller brought a case against the then government, claiming that it could not proceed with the next stage of its Brexit plans following the referendum vote to leave the EU, without an act of Parliament.

In 2017, the Supreme Court ruling in favour of Gina Miller, drew on the 1610 case of proclamations in making its decision. So even the oldest of court decisions still have power to influence justice today.

29 Discuss how this ruling is a good example of the application of common law. (AO2) **4 marks**

....
....
....
....
....

30 Examine the case for retaining common law as an essential element of the UK system of justice. (AO3) **8 marks**

....
....
....
....
....
....
....
....
....
....
....

The right to representation

31 Name an example of an employers' association. (AO1) **1 mark**

....

32 Using case studies, justify the existence of trade unions. (AO3)   **8 marks**

....

....

....

....

....

....

....

....

....

....

The nature of criminality in the UK today

33 Name an example of a crime that is associated with the term 'fraud'. (AO1)   **1 mark**

....

Source C: Courts deal with three categories of offences

> 1 **Summary only offences** – these are the least serious offences and are largely dealt with by the Magistrates' Court.
>
> 2 **Either way offences** – more serious offences. With these cases, magistrates have to decide whether or not they are too serious for them to deal with, and if their sentencing powers are sufficient if the person pleads, or is found, guilty.
>
> 3 **Indictable only offences** – these are the most serious offences. The accused will first appear in a Magistrates' Court, but then be referred to the Crown Court. Often the police will have refused to grant bail and the first hearing takes place when the person is in custody.

34 For any **two** of **three** categories outlined in **Source C**, discuss why a specific offence would fall within its remit. (AO2)   **4 marks**

Category: ....   Offence: ....

....

....

....

Category: ....   Offence: ....

....

....

....

35 Evaluate the problems for law enforcement agencies regarding dealing with increasing levels of cybercrime. (AO3)

8 marks

....

....

....

....

....

....

....

....

....

....

....

Source D: Sentencing of males and females

The average custodial sentence length for male offenders in 2017 was 17.6 months, and 10.0 months for females. This difference is due to the higher proportion of female offenders receiving shorter sentences.

On 30 June 2018:

- 22 per cent of females in prison were serving determinate sentences of less than 12 months, compared to 9 per cent of males.
- 15 per cent of females in prison were serving determinate sentences of less than 6 months, compared to 6 per cent for males.

36 Discuss why women are likely to serve shorter sentences than men. (AO2)

4 marks

....

....

....

....

....

37 Examine the reasons why under 18-year-olds, who make up only a tenth of the population, are responsible for 23 per cent of offences. (AO3)

8 marks

....

....

....

....

....

....

....

....

....

....

38 Which **two** incidents in the list below would be described as anti-social behaviour offences? (AO1)

2 marks

Shade in the **two** correct answers.

A   Shoplifting

B   Vandalism

C   Driving a vehicle without insurance

D   Fly-posting

E   Common assault

Source E: Neighbourhood Watch Schemes

Maunders Neighbourhood Watch group was formed in about 2017, following a series of break-ins, during which both vehicles and household property were stolen. At first, signs were set up throughout the area and then, in 2019, the group decided to install CCTV and signs to indicate that CCTV was in operation in order to increase security and give peace of mind. The cost was kept down significantly as every household bought into the scheme. There are two co-ordinators who work in the area, both approved and vetted by the local police.

39 Describe **two** benefits to a community of setting up a Neighbourhood Watch Scheme. (AO2)

4 marks

1   ....

....

....

2   ....

....

....

40 If you were the Home Secretary, what changes would you introduce to reduce crime in the UK? Justify your answer. (AO3)

8 marks

....

....

....

....

....

....

....

....

....

How we deal with those who commit crime

41 Identify an example of a punishment linked to each of the following terms: (AO1)   **2 marks**

Custodial sentence: ....

....

Non-custodial sentence: ....

....

Source F: Life on death row

In the USA there are approximately 2,900 prisoners awaiting execution. The death penalty is legal in 31 states. The most common method to carry out the execution is lethal injection. Prisoners often spend many years on death row awaiting execution – the average length of time is more than 15 years. Some are still waiting after 20 and even 40 years. This extended wait can be for numerous reasons including the appeals process.

42 Consider **one** argument put forward by those who support the death penalty and **one** by those opposed to the death penalty. (AO2)   **4 marks**

In favour of the death penalty:

....

....

....

Against the use of the death penalty:

....

....

....

43 Many people argue that community sentences are the best way to deal with people who commit some crimes. Evaluate the case either for **or** against this point of view. (AO3) **8 marks**

....

....

....

....

....

....

....

....

....

....

Source G: Life sentences

If a person is found guilty of murder, a court must give them a life sentence. A court may choose to give a life sentence for other serious offences like rape or armed robbery.

A life sentence lasts for the rest of a person's life – if they are released from prison after serving the minimum years set they can be recalled to prison at any time if it is felt they are a danger to the public.

A whole-life term means there is no minimum term set by the judge, and the person is never considered for release.

44 Consider **one** argument in favour of the 'whole-life means life' policy described in **Source G** and **one** argument against this policy. (AO2) **4 marks**

Argument for: ....

....

....

Argument against: ....

....

....

45 In 2003, the Criminal Justice Act stated that there were five purposes of sentencing. If you were re-drafting this Act today, offering justifications, what do you think should be the purposes of sentencing? (AO3) **8 marks**

....

....

....

....

....

....

....

....

....

....

46 What is meant by the term 're-offending'? (AO1) **2 marks**

....

....

Source H: Community sentences

According to the government:

- You may get a community sentence if you are convicted of a crime by a court, but are not sent to prison.
- You may have to do unpaid work in your local community, like removing graffiti. This is called Community Payback.

Community sentences can be given for crimes such as:

- damaging property
- benefit fraud
- assault.

47 Describe **two** circumstances when a court is likely to give a person found guilty a community sentence. (AO2) **4 marks**

1 ....

....

....

2 ....

....

....

48 Analyse the arguments put forward by those who say that prison doesn't work. (AO3) **8 marks**

....

....

....

....

....

....

....

....

....

....

How the youth justice system operates

Source I: Youth crime

> Recently a 12-year-old boy was found to have sent racist text messages to a black premier league football player. The police arrested the boy. The boy will appear before a youth court.

49 What points would you consider if you were the magistrate determining the boy's sentence? (AO2)　　　　　　　　　　　　　　　**4 marks**

....

....

....

....

....

50 Justify the reasons why youth courts operate differently than other courts. (AO3)　　**8 marks**

....

....

....

....

....

....

....

....

....

....

....

What are the universal human rights and how do we protect them?

Practice questions

The importance of key international agreements and treaties

Source A: Preamble to the Universal Declaration of Human Rights

Whereas recognition of the inherent dignity and of the equal and inalienable rights of all members of the human family is the foundation of freedom, justice and peace in the world,

Whereas disregard and contempt for human rights have resulted in barbarous acts which have outraged the conscience of mankind, and the advent of a world in which human beings shall enjoy freedom of speech and belief and freedom from fear and want has been proclaimed as the highest aspiration of the common people,

Whereas it is essential, if man is not to be compelled to have recourse, as a last resort, to rebellion against tyranny and oppression, that human rights should be protected by the rule of law,

Whereas it is essential to promote the development of friendly relations between nations, …

51 Discuss the historical context in which the preamble (introduction) above was drafted. (AO2)

4 marks

....
....
....
....
....

52 Examine why some people argue that the UN Declaration on Human Rights is dated and no longer fit for purpose. (AO3)

8 marks

....
....
....
....
....
....
....
....
....

53 Which body is responsible for establishing the European Convention on Human Rights? (AO1)   1 mark

....

Source B: The UK and the ECHR

> According to European Court data, there have been 547 judgments concerning the UK up to the end of 2018. Of these, over half (315) found were found to violate at least one Article of the European Convention on Human Rights and about a quarter (141) did not violate the Convention. The following are two examples of cases where the UK government has been found to contravene the Convention.
> - Insufficient protection of confidential journalist material under electronic surveillance schemes: breach of Article 10.
> - Ineffective investigation into death of relative at the hands of Northern Ireland security forces: breach of Article 2.1.

54 Consider the route through the UK judicial system that led to these cases coming before the European Court of Human Rights. (AO2)   4 marks

....

....

....

....

....

....

55 Examine the benefits to a citizen living in a country that is signed up to the European Convention on Human Rights. (AO3)   8 marks

....

....

....

....

....

....

....

....

....

....

....

56 Which body is responsible for the Convention on the Rights of the Child? (AO1)   1 mark

....

57 Justify why you believe there is a need for an international convention regarding the rights of children. (AO1)   8 marks

....

....

....

....

....

....

....

....

....

....

....

....

58 Identify the international court to which UK citizens can appeal if they think their human rights have been violated. (AO1)   1 mark

....

Source C: Human Rights Act, 1998

The Human Rights Act (HRA) 1998, incorporated the European Convention on Human Rights (ECHR) into UK law.

Two sections of the ECHR were omitted from the HRA (1998): Articles 1 and 13.

- Article 1 says that states must secure the rights of the Convention in their own jurisdiction.
- Article 13 says if people's rights are violated they are able to access effective remedy.

59 Describe how the Human Rights Act (1998) enables UK citizens to say that neither of these articles is required. (AO2)   4 marks

....

....

....

....

....

60 Evaluate how the Human Rights Act, 1998, improved the rights of UK citizens. (AO3)

8 marks

....

....

....

....

....

....

....

....

....

....

....

The role of international law in conflict situations

61 Which international body is the guardian of the Geneva Convention? (AO1)

1 mark

....

Source D: Alleged war crimes in Syria

According to Amnesty International, numerous war crimes have been committed in the Syrian civil war. These include attacks on residential areas, including a school, and a summary killing of a prominent politician. There have also been military attacks that have involved the use of chemical agents in residential areas. Many civilians have been forced to flee their homes due to the constant fear of indiscriminate bombing.

62 Describe how the events in **Source D** can be said to be war crimes. (AO2)

4 marks

....

....

....

....

....

....

Synoptic question

The last 8-mark question at the end of each of the three themes is a synoptic question. The question aims to draw upon your knowledge and understanding across different parts of the specification.

63 Some politicians believe that the judiciary should be brought under political control.

Considering a range of evidence and points of view, to what extent do you agree or disagree with the statement? (AO3)   **8 marks**

In your answer you should consider:

- how the judiciary currently operates
- the degree to which politicians do and could control the judicial process.

Example student answer

In the UK the judiciary is independent of government and politics. In recent years, with changes in legislation and the establishment of the Supreme Court, judges have become more involved in making judgments about the actions of government.

The case for greater political control can be made based upon the concept of public accountability. All politicians under the system are subject to re-election, so if citizens are not happy with the political control of judges they can vote the politicians out of office. Also, we as citizens can complain to our politicians and ensure that judges make decisions that suit public opinion. In the USA, many judges are directly elected and therefore are accountable to the public.

The case against political control is that in a free society it is important that there is a branch of government that is non-political and independent, so that the public know it can hold government to account through the court system. During the Brexit situation, the government was forced to a have a parliamentary vote and was unable to close down Parliament due to citizens taking judicial action.

It is an important element of the UK constitution that we have an independent judiciary that provides continuity. If there was political control over appointments as governments change, judges might be changed and new views be expressed about our laws.

> **AO3:** The response tackles both sides of the argument, makes a number of valid points and includes a comparative example. Political control and the role of citizens are discussed and the response includes useful examples of judicial activity. The response comes to a clear conclusion. Awarded 8 marks.

Paper 2, Section B: Rights and responsibilities

1 How many magistrates sit together to form the bench in a court?
Shade in the **one** correct answer.   1 mark

A   2   ⬭

B   3   ⬭

C   4   ⬭

D   12 ⬭

2 Explain what is meant by the phrase 'a majority decision' by a jury.   2 marks

....

....

Source A: Jury or no jury trails

> In the 1970s, during 'the Troubles' in Northern Ireland, trials were held without juries.
> Judges decided guilt or innocence and any sentence. In recent years, some have called
> for the end of jury trials as many cases are claimed to be too complex for juries to
> understand.

3 Discuss **two** reasons why jury trails, as described in **Source A**, could not take place during
'the Troubles' in Northern Ireland.   4 marks

1 ....

....

....

....

2 ....

....

....

4 Explain what is meant by 'common law'.   1 mark

....

5 Name the **two** police forces that operate in London.   2 marks

....

....

Source B: Powers of the police

The police are often criticised in the media in regard to issues surrounding stop and search and the way, it is claimed, they go about arresting people. The way the police operate is governed by the law.

6   Referring to **Source B**, describe **two** actions the police **have** to undertake when arresting someone.   **4 marks**

1   ....

....

....

2   ....

....

....

7   Define what is meant by a 'suspended sentence'.   **1 mark**

....

....

8   Re-offending is a serious issue for the criminal justice system. Evaluate the options open to society to try to reduce the re-offending rate in the UK.   **8 marks**

....

....

....

....

....

....

....

....

....

....

9   Identify **one** benefit of the European arrest warrant system.   **1 mark**

....

....

10 Explain what is meant by 'stop and search'.   **2 marks**

....

....

Source C: Tribunals and ombudsmen

> Tribunals and the ombudsman systems were designed to make access to resolving complaints and issues easier and less expensive for citizens.

11 Referring to **Source C**, describe **one** issue or complaint you could refer to a named tribunal and **one** you could refer to a named ombudsman.   **4 marks**

Tribunal: ....

....

Complaint: ....

....

Ombudsman: ....

....

Complaint: ....

....

....

12 Which **one** of the following rights is acquired at the age of 13?   **1 mark**
   Shade in the **one** correct answer.

   A   You can choose your own religion.   ⬭

   B   You may be remanded to a prison to await trial.   ⬭

   C   You can have a Facebook account.   ⬭

   D   You reach the age of criminal responsibility.   ⬭

13 Which **two** parts of the UK have identical legal systems?   **2 marks**
   Shade in the **two** correct answers.

   A   England   ⬭

   B   Scotland   ⬭

   C   Wales   ⬭

   D   Northern Ireland   ⬭

Source D: Civil and criminal cases

> Civil and criminal cases can proceed in different courts and the outcomes are different. A divorce case in a civil court is entirely different from someone being tried for murder. But both cases heard within courts in the UK share some common principles.

14 Comparing civil court cases and criminal court cases as outlined in **Source D**, describe **two** shared legal principles or procedures.　　　　　4 marks

1 ....

....

....

2 ....

....

....

15 Identify how common law is created.　　　　　1 mark

....

....

16 Analyse a case for **not** abolishing the 1998 Human Rights Act.　　　　　8 marks

....

....

....

....

....

....

....

....

....

....

....

....

17 In which year was the Universal Declaration on Human Rights agreed?　　　　　1 mark
Shade in the **one** correct answer.

A　1945　　⬭

B　1948　　⬭

C　1951　　⬭

D　1960　　⬭

18 The 'burden of proof' differs in a civil case and a criminal case. Explain how the term is used in each type of case. 2 marks

Civil case: ....

....

Criminal case: ....

....

Source E: Employers' associations

The list below is the first ten employers' associations listed on the government's official registration website:

- Advertising Producers Association
- Association of British Orchestras
- Association of Circus Proprietors of Great Britain
- Association of Indian Banks in the United Kingdom
- Association of Newspaper and Magazine Wholesalers

- Association of Plumbing and Heating Contractors
- British Amusement Catering Trades Association
- British Lace Federation
- British Printing Industries Federation
- Builders Merchants Federation Ltd

19 Describe any **two** functions that are carried out by employers' associations. Link your answer to any **two** associations from **Source E**. 4 marks

Association: .... Function: ....

....

....

....

Association: .... Function: ....

....

....

....

20 What do the initials YOT stand for? 1 mark

....

21 Define what is meant by 'rehabilitation' when it is used in regard to sentencing. 2 marks

....

....

....

....

Source F: House of Lords Report on the Rights of Children, 2015

> We do have concerns that, unlike her counterparts in Northern Ireland, Scotland and Wales, the Commissioner is not empowered to take up individual cases on behalf of children. We accept that granting these powers to the Children's Commissioner for England would need to go hand-in-hand with a possibly significant increase in resources.

22 Referring to **Source F**, consider **two** benefits to children in England if the proposal from the House of Lords was implemented.   **4 marks**

1 ....

....

....

2 ....

....

....

23 Of the total number of court convictions in England and Wales in 2017, which of the following was the correct ratio between females and males?   **1 mark**

Shade in the **one** correct answer.

	Females %	Males %	
A	10	90	⬭
B	25	75	⬭
C	35	65	⬭
D	50	50	⬭
E	60	40	⬭

24 Analyse the extent to which it can be claimed that the International Criminal Court has been successful since it was set up in 1998.   **8 marks**

....

....

....

....

....

....

....

....

....

....

Theme 3 Politics and participation

This theme covers the nature of political power and government in the UK and the values and institutions of a democracy. It looks at the structure and role of local and devolved governments, voting systems and the organisation of parliament and government. Finally, it looks at how MEPs are elected in the EU and the differences between a democratic and non-democratic society. The Active Citizenship element of this theme is covered in Theme 4.

Where does political power reside in the UK and how is it controlled?

The concept of democracy

1 Which of the following describes the UK system of government? (AO1)   **1 mark**
   Shade in the **one** correct answer.

   A   Dictatorship   ⬭

   B   Direct democracy   ⬭

   C   One-party state   ⬭

   D   Representative democracy   ⬭

   E   Totalitarian   ⬭

Source A: System of government in Saudi Arabia

> The governmental system in Saudi Arabia is based upon the principle of absolute monarchy, where the monarch must govern based on Islamic principles. Decisions are largely taken on the basis of debate among the senior princes of the royal family and leading religious clerics. The king, as well as being head of state, is also the head of the government.

2 Outline **two** ways in which the UK is governed differently from Saudi Arabia. (AO2)   **4 marks**

1 ....

....

....

....

2 ....

....

....

....

3   According to Sir Winston Churchill in 1947:

'Democracy is the worst form of government except all those other forms that have been tried from time to time.'

Analyse the case for democracy being the best form of government for a modern society. (AO3)   **8 marks**

....
....
....
....
....
....
....
....
....
....
....

The values underpinning democracy

4   Give **one** example of a current piece of legislation relating to equality in the UK. (AO1)   **1 mark**

....

Source B: Human rights abuses in North Korea

The government in North Korea does not allow political opposition, an independent media, a civil society or trade unions. The state operates secret prison camps where prisoners face torture. A UN Commission of Inquiry found that the North Korean government commits widespread rights abuse.

5   Explain why the UK government does not act in the same way as the North Korean government. (AO2)   **4 marks**

Example student answer

The UK government is accountable to Parliament, the courts and its citizens at the ballot box. The rule of law is supreme in the UK, the government cannot break the law and it can be held to account for its actions. Also, in the UK, we have a free press and media who can report on the actions of the government, and increasingly citizens through social media hold the government to account for what it does.

AO2: The response covers a range of points about accountability in the UK and identifies how the government is held to account. More than sufficient for 4 marks.

6　Evaluate the case for making voting in elections compulsory in the UK. (AO3)　　8 marks

....

....

....

....

....

....

....

....

....

....

....

The institutions of the British constitution

7　Which **two** of the following posts are held by a UK Prime Minister? (AO1)　　2 marks
Shade in the **two** correct answers.

A　First Lord of the Treasury

B　MEP

C　MP

D　Councillor

E　Queens Counsel

F　Lord Chancellor

8　'Parliament is all powerful within the UK system of government.'
Analyse the extent to which this statement is correct. (AO3)　　8 marks

Example student answer

Within our system of government, Parliament is the supreme body. Only it can pass or amend laws, agree levels of taxation and recently it was agreed that it can decide whether our armed forces are used in a conflict. Over time many would now say that the concept has been eroded and now government, rather than Parliament, is more powerful. Ministers have the power to make major changes without votes in Parliament. A government, like that of Boris Johnson elected in 2019 with a majority of over 80, is very powerful due to the strength of the party system to ensure MPs vote following the party line.

Some years ago it was stated by a leading politician that we actually lived in an 'elected dictatorship' where not just the government was all powerful but the Prime Minister was all powerful within government. As was seen during the Brexit crisis from 2016 to 2019, Parliament can take control, until 2019 when a general election gave the government a very large majority. So much depends on the nature of the make-up of Parliament to say it is all powerful; in theory it can control government, but if a government has a large majority it can be very difficult to exercise that power.

AO3: The response shows a very clear understanding of the concepts relating to parliamentary power. The use of a contemporary example helps to support the argument. Points are further developed regarding the power of government and Prime Ministerial power. Clear concluding points. Awarded 8 marks.

The relationships between the institutions

9   The UK is said to have an unwritten constitution. Explain what is meant by this. (AO1)　　　　2 marks

....
....
....
....

Source C: Supreme Court

Until 2005, the highest court in the UK was the House of Lords, where the Law Lords heard cases. In 2005, the Constitutional Reform Act established a Supreme Court for the United Kingdom to ensure that judicial decisions were separate from those of Parliament and the government.

10   Describe why it is important for the highest court in the United Kingdom to be separate from Parliament. (AO2)　　　　4 marks

....
....
....
....
....
....

What are the powers of local and devolved government and how can citizens participate?

The role and structure of elected local government

Source A: Local government needs to cut services

> Your local council has to make £500,000 of cuts to services this year to balance its budget. This is a legal requirement and it cannot borrow additional funds or raise its council tax.

11 Describe which **two** service cuts you would make. Explain your decision. (AO2)   **4 marks**

1 ....

....

....

2 ....

....

....

12 Examine the case made for having directly elected mayors. (AO3)   **8 marks**

....

....

....

....

....

....

....

....

....

....

The nature and organisation of regional and devolved government

13 Identify which part of the UK has a directly elected parliament. (AO1)   **1 mark**
Shade in the **one** correct answer.

A   England

B   Scotland

C   Wales

D   Northern Ireland

14 Justify a case for more **or** less devolution within the UK. (AO3)   8 marks

....

....

....

....

....

....

....

....

....

....

....

How powers are organised

15 Name **one** part of the UK that has a directly elected assembly. (AO1)   1 mark

....

Source B: The German federal system of government

The division of power is a basic element of the German federal constitution.

Each Länder (regional state) has its own prime minister, parliament and powers.

The central government and the federation work together within a system of checks and balances. The individual regional state also participates in decisions made by the national government by having members in the Bundesrat (Upper House of the Federal Parliament).

16 Compare the system described in **Source B** with the relationship between the UK government and the devolved bodies in the UK. (AO2)   4 marks

....

....

....

....

....

....

17 Analyse the case for establishing an English Parliament while still retaining the UK Parliament. (AO3)

....
....
....
....
....
....
....
....
....
....

Who can stand for election and how candidates are selected

Source C: 'A-list' candidates

The Conservative Party some years ago decided to create an 'A-list' of candidates to become MPs. These were people from a range of non-political backgrounds, including business, the media and entertainment. They were young and contained a high number of women and people from a BAME background. Certain local constituency parties were encouraged to select candidates from this list.

18 Consider **one** and advantage and **one** disadvantage of the 'A-list' system. (AO2)   4 marks

Advantage: ....

....

....

Disadvantage: ....

....

....

19 Justify the arguments put forward by political parties when selecting candidates from women-only lists. (AO3)

8 marks

....
....
....
....
....

....

....

....

....

....

Who can and cannot vote in elections and why

20 Identify **one** group of adults who live in the United Kingdom but are not allowed to vote in the UK General Election. (AO1)

1 mark

....

Source D: Voting ages

> In the Scottish independence referendum, 16-year-olds were allowed to vote. In the European Union membership referendum, you had to be at least 18 years old in order to vote. To vote in a UK General Election you have to be 18. You can vote in local elections in Scotland and Wales at 16, but in England and Northern Ireland you must be 18.

21 Consider **one** argument in favour of voting at 16 and **one** in favour of voting at 18. (AO2)

4 marks

At 16: ....

....

....

At 18: ....

....

....

22 Justify the arguments put forward supporting the rights of prisoners to vote in elections. (AO3)

8 marks

....

....

....

....

....

....

....

....

....

....

....

Issues relating to voting

23 Define what is meant by 'voter turnout'. (AO1)   **1 mark**

....

Source E: 100 per cent postal vote elections

Due to the pandemic in 2020, many American states are considering introducing a full postal vote election for the November 2020, elections, which include the election of the President of the United States. The current President, Donald Trump, opposes this as he believes this will not assist his re-election. In the UK, 100 per cent postal voting has been tried in some local elections on a trial basis.

24 Describe **one** claimed advantage and **one** disadvantage of 100 per cent postal vote elections. (AO2)   **4 marks**

Advantage: ....

....

....

Disadvantage: ....

....

25 Analyse the validity and likely success of any **two** suggestions put forward to increase voter turnout at elections. (AO3)   **8 marks**

....

....

....

....

....

....

....

....

....

....

How public taxes are raised and spent by government

26 Which of the **two** following taxes are taken from the wage packets of employees? (AO1)   **2 marks**

Shade in the **two** correct answers.

A   Income tax

B   VAT

C   National Insurance

D   Council tax

E   Excise duty

Source F: Government tax revenues

> The UK government raises its income to pay for public services from a range of sources such as: income tax, National Insurance, business rates, VAT and duties on goods like alcohol and tobacco.

27 Consider an advantage and a disadvantage of raising or lowering any one of the taxes mentioned in **Source F**. (AO2)   **4 marks**

Choice of tax: ....

....

Advantage: ....

....

....

....

Disadvantage: ....

....

....

....

28 Justify a case for either increasing or cutting one major area of central government spending. (AO3)   **8 marks**

....

....

....

....

....

....

....

....

....

....

The way the government makes decisions about its spending: the factors they take into account

Source G: Heathrow Airport third runway proposal

For many years the government has promoted the idea that Heathrow Airport needs a third runway. Many oppose this for a range of reasons and it is very unpopular in the area where it would be built. Those in favour, argue that it is a major infrastructure programme that is needed to boost the UK economy and that other areas of the country would benefit economically.

29 Discuss **one** argument that could be put forward by those opposed to this project. (AO2)

4 marks

....

....

....

....

....

....

30 During the 2020 pandemic, the government borrowed hundreds of billions of additional pounds. Examine why the government took such action. (AO3)

8 marks

....

....

....

....

....

....

....

....

....

....

Debates about provision for welfare, health, the elderly and education

31 Define, using an example, what is meant by the term 'welfare benefit'. (AO1)   **2 marks**

....

....

....

....

32 The National Health Service is provided free of charge at the point of delivery.

Examine the case for changing the way the NHS is funded to an insurance policy system, paid for directly by individuals. (AO3)   **8 marks**

....

....

....

....

....

....

....

....

....

....

....

....

Where does political power reside: with the citizen, parliament or government?

The 'first past the post' system

Source A: Results in Constituencies A and B

Constituency A	Constituency B
Conservative 38,955	Labour 21,348
Liberal Democrat 15,342	Conservative 19,352
Labour 9,689	Liberal Democrat 13,490
Green Party 2,346	Green Party 3,509

33 **Source A** indicates the results in two different constituencies. How can the result in one be used by supporters of the 'first past the post' system and how can the result in the other be used by those who oppose the 'first past the post' system? (AO2)

4 marks

Argument for: ....

....

....

Argument against: ....

....

....

34 Analyse the arguments put for and against fixed-term Parliaments. (AO3)   **8 marks**

....

....

....

....

....

....

....

....

....

....

....

....

Other voting systems used in the UK

35 Name **one** proportional voting system used in public elections in the UK. (AO1)   1 mark

....

Source B: The election of directly elected mayors

> The system used to elect directly elected mayors allows voters to have a first and second choice. The winning candidate has to have over 50 per cent of the vote to win. Candidates with the lowest number of votes are eliminated and their second votes are transferred.

36 Describe how the system outlined in **Source B** differs from a proportional electoral system. (AO2)   4 marks

....

....

....

....

....

....

37 Justify a case for keeping the 'first past the post' electoral system for electing Members of Parliament in the UK. (AO3)   8 marks

....

....

....

....

....

....

....

....

....

....

....

The executive, the legislature and the judiciary

38 Identify the term that appears before 'monarchy' to describe the role of the monarchy in the UK. (AO1)

1 mark

....

Source C: The UK system of government

> The UK relies upon three key components of government in order to function and provide a system of checks and balances: Parliament, the executive and the judiciary.

39 Describe **one** way in which any of the three components of government mentioned in **Source C** are linked and **one** way in which any two are independent of each other. (AO2)

4 marks

Linked: ....

....

....

Independent: ....

....

....

40 For many years there have been proposals to reform the membership of the House of Lords and the way members are appointed.

Analyse the case against having a directly elected House of Lords. (AO3)

8 marks

....

....

....

....

....

....

....

....

....

....

....

....

....

The major political parties in the UK

41 Which **two** of the following political parties only contest elections in Northern Ireland? (AO1)

Shade in the **two** correct answers.

2 marks

A SDLP

B SNP

C UUP

D PC

E DUP

F Lib Dems

Source D: Slogans

The following are slogans used by political parties in the 2019 UK General Election:

1 Get Brexit Done

2 Stop Brexit – Build a brighter future

3 It's time to choose our own future

4 NHS not for sale

42 Select **two** of the slogans and state with which party they are associated. For each, give a reason for your choice. (AO2)

4 marks

Slogan and party: ....

....

Reason: ....

....

....

Slogan and party: ....

....

Reason: ....

....

....

43 Analyse the key differences between the Conservative Party and the Labour Party in any **two** important policy areas. (AO3)

8 marks

....

....

....

....

....

....

....

....

....

....

....

How parliament works

44 Explain the work a parliamentary select committee undertakes. (AO1)

1 mark

....

....

Source E: Parliamentary time

Most of the time for debates in the House of Commons is controlled by the government, but some days are allocated as opposition days where the opposition can decide the topic to be debated.

45 If you were the Leader of the Opposition, what would be your choice of a motion for debate on an opposition day and why would you choose this topic for debate? (AO2)

4 marks

Opposition motion: ....

....

....

....

Reason for your choice: ....

....

....

....

46 Examine the case for retaining Prime Minister's Question Time every week in its current format. (AO3)

8 marks

....

....

....

....

....

....

....

....

....

....

....

The role of Members of Parliament (MPs)

Source F: Airport closure scenario

You are an MP, who is contacted by your local council about the closure of the nearby airport after the collapse of an airline that was a major employer at the airport. The council is one of the main shareholders in the airport, and the airport is one of the largest employers in this semi-rural area.

47 In regard to the specific issue in **Source F**, describe **two** actions you could take as local MP to try to find a solution to the situation. (AO2)

4 marks

1 ....

....

....

2 ....

....

....

48 Members of Parliament are able to promote new laws through Private Member's Bills. If you were an MP, justify the case for a Private Member's Bill you would like to introduce. (AO3)

8 marks

....

....

....

....

....

....

....

....

....

....

Ceremonial roles and key parliamentary roles

Source G: Members of Parliament

MPs start their political careers as backbench MPs – seated on the back benches of the House of Commons. Many aspire to become frontbench MPs – sitting on the front benches, either side of the table.

49 Discuss **one** advantage of being a backbencher and **one** of being a frontbencher. (AO2) **4 marks**

Backbencher: ....

....

....

Frontbencher: ....

....

....

50 Examine the methods used by political parties in the House of Commons to ensure that their MPs vote along party lines. (AO3) **8 marks**

....

....

....

....

....

....

....

....

....

....

....

The legislative process

Source H: E-petitions

The UK government has an e-petition system whereby members of the public can raise issues online that they wish Parliament to debate. For the proposal to be considered for debate, 100,000 people must support it online.

51 Consider **one** strength and **one** weakness of the e-petition system. (AO2)   **4 marks**

Strength: ....

....

....

....

Weakness: ....

....

....

....

52 Examine the role of the House of Commons in the legislative process. (AO3)   **8 marks**

....

....

....

....

....

....

....

....

....

....

....

....

Government formation

53 In 2020, what was the minimum number of seats needed by a political party in order to be able to win a General Election and form a majority government? (AO1)   *1 mark*

Shade in the **one** correct answer.

A   200   ◯

B   226   ◯

C   301   ◯

D   326   ◯

E   650   ◯

Source I: Formation of a government

As soon as a majority is achieved in a General Election, a newly appointed Prime Minister has to start appointing the main government ministers.

54 Discuss which **four** major cabinet posts you would appoint at the start of forming a government, and give a reason for your choices. (AO2)   *4 marks*

1 ....   3 ....

2 ....   4 ....

Reason for these choices: ....

....

....

....

55 Evaluate the strengths and weaknesses of coalition governments. (AO3)   *8 marks*

....

....

....

....

....

....

....

....

....

....

....

The role of the Prime Minister, cabinet and ministers

56 Which **two** of the following office holders are members of the cabinet? (AO1)   **2 marks**
Shade in the **two** correct answers.

A   First Lord of the Treasury

B   The Lord Speaker

C   Home Secretary

D   Black Rod

E   Serjeant at Arms

F   Leader of the Opposition

57 The following expression is often used to describe the role of a Prime Minister within the UK cabinet government system: 'first among equals'.

Evaluate to what extent this is an accurate statement. (AO3)   **8 marks**

....

....

....

....

....

....

....

....

....

....

....

The organisation of government administration

Source J: A new US President

When a new President comes into office, as well as appointing senior members of the administration (ministers), they also have to appoint over 4,000 senior officials and administrators from Ambassadors, to what we know as senior civil servants. All of this is done by a special transition team appointed by the new President, after their election in November. Most of these posts have to be filled by the following January. Many posts are given to political supporters of the President and many are filled by financial donors to the campaign.

58 Describe how the transition to a new government differs in the UK. (AO2)   4 marks

....

....

....

....

....

59 Over recent years, the number of civil servants in the UK has declined, while more government services are provided by government agencies.

Assess the arguments for and against public services being provided through agency arrangements. (AO3)   8 marks

....

....

....

....

....

....

....

....

....

....

....

How do others govern themselves?

Electoral systems and processes used in European parliamentary elections

Source K: The UK Parliament

In the UK Parliament, in the House of Commons, the political parties face each other across the chamber. On one side, there is the government and on the other, the opposition parties. If a Member of Parliament leaves their party, to join an opposing one, it is known as 'crossing the floor' as they literally have to cross the floor of the chamber to move parties.

60 Compare the layout and party structure of the European Parliament with that of the House of Commons. (AO2)

4 marks

....
....
....
....
....

61 The elections to the European Union (EU) Parliament, which take place in each EU member country, have to use a system of proportional voting.

Evaluate the advantages of using a proportional system for elections to the EU Parliament. (AO3)

8 marks

....
....
....
....
....
....
....
....
....
....

Democratic and non-democratic political systems

Source L: One-party state

Some countries in the world, for example China, Cuba, Eritrea, Laos, Vietnam and the Western Sahara, are governed by a single party and that is the only political party that is allowed in the country. These countries may hold elections but only allow candidates from the ruling party to stand.

62 Consider **two** reasons why one-party states are not considered to be democratic. (AO2)

4 marks

1 ....

....

....

2 ....

....

....

Synoptic question

The last 8-mark question at the end of each of the three themes is a synoptic question. The question aims to draw upon your knowledge and understanding across different parts of the specification.

63 'Giving more powers to the nations and regions of the United Kingdom will led to the break-up of the UK as a nation state and will mean the end of the values that underpin British society.'

To what extent do you agree or disagree with this statement?

In your answer you should consider:

- the nature of power sharing within the UK
- what is meant by shared British values. (AO3)

8 marks

....

....

....

....

....

....

....

....

....

....

....

Paper 1, Section C: Politics and participation

1 How many countries make up the United Kingdom?   1 mark
   Shade in the **one** correct answer.

   A   1

   B   3

   C   4

   D   5

2 Explain why the House of Commons is more powerful than the House
   of Lords.   2 marks

   ....

   ....

   ....

   ....

Source A: Local government reform

The government is proposing that lots of local councils merge into larger unitary
authorities, each with a population of at least about 800,000. This means that existing
County and District Councils will disappear. The government also wants each of these
new councils to be run by a directly elected mayor.

3 Using **Source A**, consider **one** argument in favour of setting up these new
   unitary authorities and **one** argument against.   4 marks

   Argument for: ....

   ....

   ....

   ....

   ....

   Argument against: ....

   ....

   ....

   ....

   ....

4 Name the voting system used in the UK to elect MPs to the House of Commons.   1 mark

   ....

5 Define the term 'cabinet government'. 2 marks

....

....

....

....

Source B: Voter turnout in recent elections and referendums

General Election	68.7%
EU Referendum	72.0%
Referendum on Scottish Independence	84.6%
Local government elections	31.3%

6 Referring to **Source B**, consider why more people turn out to vote in referendums than in elections. 4 marks

....

....

....

....

....

....

7 Name the title given to the head of government in the UK. 1 mark

....

8 Evaluate the arguments in favour of and against the formation of coalition governments. 8 marks

....

....

....

....

....

....

....

....

....

....

....

9   Explain **one** change in government policy that could be announced
    in the Budget.   1 mark

....

10 Explain how the winner is decided in a constituency using the 'first past the
    post' electoral system.   2 marks

....

....

....

....

Source C: The United States of America

The USA system of government is based upon three distinct branches similar to
but different from those of the United Kingdom.

●   The Executive branch is headed by the elected President and is responsible for
    enforcing laws passed by Congress. The President is also the Head of State and
    Commander in Chief of the armed forces.

●   The Legislative branch, which decides upon the laws, is called Congress, and is
    split into two parts: the Senate and the House of Representatives. Both of these
    Houses are composed of elected local members.

●   The Judicial branch – the highest court in the USA – is the Supreme Court. Its
    judges are appointed by the sitting President when a vacancy arises.

11 Using **Source C**, consider **two** ways in which the UK institutions of government
    differ from that of the USA.   4 marks

1   ....

....

....

....

2   ....

....

....

....

12 Which **one** of the following local councils has the most powers?   1 mark
    Shade in the **one** correct answer.

    A   District

    B   County

    C   Unitary

    D   Parish

13 Identify **two** ways in which an MP can try to change legislation as it passes through Parliament. 2 marks

1 ....

....

2 ....

....

Source D: Devolution in the UK

The individual nations of the UK have different powers and responsibilities granted to them by the UK Parliament.

14 Using **Source D**, discuss **two** reasons for the varying pattern of devolution in the UK. 4 marks

1 ....

....

....

2 ....

....

....

15 Identify the minimum age at which someone can stand for election to the UK Parliament. 1 mark

Shade in the **one** correct answer.

A   16   ⬭

B   18   ⬭

C   20   ⬭

D   21   ⬭

16 Evaluate the case for the UK, like many other countries, having a written constitution contained in a single codified document. 8 marks

....

....

....

....

....

....

....

....

....

....

....

17 Name the title given to the person who chairs proceedings in the House of Commons.   **1 mark**

....

18 Identify **two** of the formal stages a bill goes through before it become a law.   **2 marks**

1   ....

....

2   ....

....

Source E: Prime-ministerial power

All ministers serve at the wishes of the Prime Minister and can be dismissed by the Prime Minister at any time. Often a reshuffle of office holders is leaked to the media who then comment on who is likely to leave, be promoted and come into government.

19 Referring to **Source E**, consider **two** reasons why a Prime Minister may want to carry out a major reshuffle of their cabinet.   **4 marks**

1   ....

....

....

2   ....

....

20 What is meant by the term 'transnational political group' in regard to the EU?   **1 mark**

....

21 Explain, using **one** example, what is meant by the term 'government agency'.   **2 marks**

....

....

....

....

Source F: Working tax credits

People in low-paid work are supported by the government through the tax credit system, which in effect increases their take-home pay.

22 Referring to **Source F**, consider **one** advantage and **one** disadvantage of the working tax credit system.   **4 marks**

Advantage: ....

....

....

....

Disadvantage: ....

....

....

....

23 State **one** indicator that means a country is non-democratic.   **1 mark**

....

24 Assess how citizens can participate in the political system in a democratic state as against a non-democratic state. Use case studies in your response.   **8 marks**

....

....

....

....

....

....

....

....

....

....

....

....

Theme 4 Active Citizenship

This theme focuses on how citizens are able to try to make a difference by their own actions. It covers both the Active Citizenship element of the three content-related themes, and the Investigation. For the content-related themes, Active Citizenship looks at understanding real-life citizenship actions and includes source-based questions. For the Investigation, you will be researching, acting and reflecting upon your own citizenship issue.

How can citizens make their voice heard and make a difference in society?

Practice questions ?

The opportunities and barriers

1   Explain what is meant by the term 'voter apathy'. (AO1)   2 marks

....

....

....

....

2   What is a petition? (AO1)   1 mark

....

....

3   Identify **one** positive and **one** negative point regarding the use of
    demonstrations to bring about change. (AO1)   2 marks

    Positive: ....

....

....

    Negative: ....

....

....

The role of organisations

4   What is a pressure group? (AO1)   1 mark

....

....

5 Identify **two** ways in which a trade union can support its members. (AO1)　　　　**2 marks**

1 ....

....

....

2 ....

....

....

How citizens work together to change communities

6 Shelter is a national charity and pressure group. Identify the area of public policy on which it campaigns. (AO1)　　　　**1 mark**

....

7 Identify **one** locally based group in your community that is attempting to bring about a change in public policy. State the name of the group and the policy issue. (AO1)　　　　**2 marks**

Name of the local group: ....

....

....

The policy issue: ....

....

....

How those who wish to bring about change use the media

8 Define what is meant by the term 'social media'. (AO1)　　　　**1 mark**

....

....

9 Identify a current local, national or international campaign and a celebrity who is associated with the campaign. (AO1)　　　　**2 marks**

The campaign: ....

....

....

The celebrity: ....

....

....

Source A: The migrant crisis

In 2016, the European Union faced a mass influx of migrants from conflicts across Africa and the Middle East. Each day, television broadcasts were full of distressing images and stories about these migrants.

The pressure group and charity Save the Children is campaigning to bring into the UK some of the children in the camps in the Middle East and Europe who have no families.

The campaign has been given a lot of media coverage. Questions have been asked in Parliament. This is a clear example of a group of charities and their supporters using the media to lobby government to bring about a change in policy, at national level.

10 Examine the reasons why campaign groups, such as Save the Children, are so successful in influencing government's actions and public opinion regarding issues like the migrant crisis.

In your response you should refer to **Source A** and examples of other groups who campaign on behalf of refugees. (AO2 and AO3)

8 marks

Worked example

Groups like Save the Children are seen as insider groups so often have the ear of government. They can contact MPs or government ministers directly and often have full-time staff working inside Parliament to influence those in government. The nature of their cause appeals to large sections of the public and it is difficult to disagree with what they are trying to achieve. They also raise a lot of funds from the public through emotive paid advertising which enables them to maintain a high profile in the media and especially on social media. Due to their status, Save the Children and other groups like the Red Cross and Médicins Sans Frontières are able to work with television reporters and gain coverage of issues that concern them. These groups are also able to enlist the support of celebrities which enables them to raise further funds.

Some other groups are actually formal international bodies like the UN Refugee Agency, UNCHR and UNICEF. By working alongside organisations such as Save the Children, these groups have become a formalised element of crisis management and are often able to intervene where governments are unable or unwilling to do so. Often such groups will be funded by governments to carry out their work.

In summary, bodies like Save the Children are able to appeal to a range of decision makers in society and also elicit widespread public support due to the nature of their cause. They have good fund-raising potential and are able to promote their cause effectively in the media.

A02 and A03: This response shows a clear understanding of the reasons behind Save the Children's success: nature of the cause, public support, insider status, working at times with government and inter-governmental agencies. Mention is made of a wide range of other bodies involved in working with migrants. The last concluding sentences provide a clear overview of the question. Awarded 8 marks.

How do citizens play a part to bring about change in the legal system?

The role of the citizen within the legal system

11 Explain what the citizen's role is as a juror. (AO1)   **1 mark**

....

....

12 Ordinary citizens can be appointed as lay magistrates. Identify **two** powers
that they exercise in a court. (AO1)   **2 marks**

1 ....

2 ....

Roles played by different groups

13 Identify **two** areas of public life where an ombudsman can investigate
complaints. (AO1)   **2 marks**

1 ....

....

....

2 ....

....

....

Different forms of democratic and citizenship actions

14 Amnesty International is often successful through its lobbying methods.
Explain what the word 'lobbying' means in this context. (AO1)   **1 mark**

....

....

15 In regard to a human rights campaign, suggest **one** democratic form of
action a citizen can take to bring about a change and give a reason for
your choice. (AO1)   **2 marks**

Democratic action: ....

....

Reason for your choice: ....

....

....

Source A: The Hillsborough disaster

On 15 April 1989, 96 Liverpool Football Club fans were crushed to death and hundreds more were injured at the Sheffield Wednesday stadium. In 1989, an inquiry by Lord Taylor found that the main cause was a failure of police crowd control. Relatives and friends did not believe that the full facts had been made public and campaigned for more information.

Twenty years later, in 2009, the Home Secretary requested that the police release all their files and they were examined by an independent group. In 2012, the group reported that the police had deliberately altered more than 160 witness statements in an attempt to blame Liverpool fans for the fatal crush.

The Prime Minister apologised as did the former editor of *The Sun* newspaper over comments the paper made at the time.

In 2012, the High Court quashed the original inquest verdicts and a fresh inquiry was held into the disaster. In 2016, 27 years after the disaster, a fresh inquest jury decided that the fans had been unlawfully killed and that the police Match Commander on the day was responsible for manslaughter by gross negligence.

16 Examine the reasons you think this campaign lasted for such a long time and why eventually it was successful.

In your response, you should refer to **Source A** and examples of any other campaigns that were successful after a long period of campaigning. (AO2 and AO3)   **8 marks**

....

....

....

....

....

....

....

....

....

....

....

How can citizens try to bring about political change?

How citizens can contribute to parliamentary democracy

17 The phrase 'lobbying' relates to the lobby in Parliament. Explain what it means when you lobby your MP. (AO1) **1 mark**

....

....

Methods of improving voter engagement

18 Define what is meant by an 'e-petition'. (AO1) **1 mark**

....

....

19 Identify **two** reasons why it is important that when the UK Parliament is in session, it is televised. (AO1) **2 marks**

1 ....

....

2 ....

....

Action to bring about political change

20 Using an example, identify what is meant by volunteering. (AO1) **1 mark**

....

....

Roles played by groups in providing a voice for society

21 Explain the role of the TUC. (AO1) **1 mark**

....

....

22 Identify **one** public institution and **one** charity that might be involved if there was an overseas emergency humanitarian crisis. (AO1) **2 marks**

Public institution: ....

....

Charity: ....

....

The Investigation: taking citizenship action

Stage 1: Deciding on the question or issue
You must select a contemporary issue/debate arising from the specification content. It can be local, national or international or a combination of all three strands. You should ask your teacher to check that the question or issue relates to the specification. Remember, the Investigation can be undertaken alone or as part of a group. Following your initial research and discussion, you construct a question/issue which you then need to research further.

Stage 2: Carrying out the initial research
You research the issue using both primary and secondary sources.

Stage 3: Planning the action
As a part of your research, you may develop further sets of questions which link to and support the main question/issue.
As a result of your research, you should be able to arrive at both results and conclusions which will help you to plan your citizenship action.

Stage 4: Taking the action
Following your research, you are expected to take some form of informed action based upon your research. This may take a variety of forms from letter writing, petitioning, using e-media, volunteering or establishing a group to promote a change.

Stage 5: Assessing the impact of the action
After taking your action you should reflect upon its impact. Did the methods used and the outcome match your expectations?

Stage 6: Evaluating the whole process
Lastly you should evaluate your whole investigative process and attempt to establish what went well and what could have been done differently.

Practice questions

1   Identify **one** primary and **one** secondary source that you used when carrying out your research. (AO1)   *2 marks*

Primary source: ....

Secondary source: ....

2   Describe how your initial research assisted you in resolving the question or issue you investigated. (AO2)   *4 marks*

....

....

....

....

....

....

3   Evaluate the strengths and weaknesses of the informed action you took after
    you completed your research. (AO1 and AO3)   6 marks

....

....

....

....

....

....

....

4   Examine the ways you could have improved your Investigation if you had additional
    time and resources.
    Your answer should refer to:
    •   the time you had available and how it was used
    •   the resources that were available
    •   what you would have undertaken if more time had been available
    •   how the availability of specific additional resources would have improved the
        Investigation. (AO2 and AO3)   12 marks

....

....

....

....

....

....

....

....

....

....

....

....

....

....

Paper 1, Section D: Active Citizenship: citizenship action

1 Identify **one** difference between a special constable and a police community support officer.   **1 mark**

....

....

2 Explain **one** reason pressure groups use social media to campaign.   **1 mark**

....

....

3 Using examples, explain the meaning of the term 'peaceful protest' in the context of active citizenship.   **2 marks**

....

....

....

....

4 Identify **two** advantages of using e-petitions rather than hand-signed petitions.   **2 marks**

1 ....

....

2 ....

....

5 Explain **one** reason why an 'insider' pressure group might be successful.   2 marks

....

....

....

....

Source A: Marcus Rashford fights for school meals

During the 2020 Covid-19 pandemic, schools were closed for much of the academic year. For many children, the midday school lunch is a very important meal. The government started a scheme, giving food vouchers to the poorest families. When the government announced the scheme would end over the summer, the Manchester United and England footballer Marcus Rashford wrote to the Prime Minister stating how important it was that the poorest had access to food. Speaking from personal experience, he explained that he had grown up in poverty so was aware of the issue many were facing. The government changed its decision and now Rashford has got together with the largest food suppliers to establish a Food Foundation to help those in need.

6 Examine why celebrities seem to be able to bring about change in society.

In your response you should refer to **Source A** and other examples of celebrities bringing about change.   8 marks

....

....

....

....

....

....

....

....

....

....

....

7   What is the title given to those people elected to serve on local authorities?   **1 mark**

....

8   Identify **one** national charity that campaigns on issues relating to the environment.   **1 mark**

....

9   Identify **two** ways in which the internet has aided public participation in the
    political process.   **2 marks**

1   ....

    ....

2   ....

....

10 Identify **two** reasons why it is important for citizens to vote in public elections.   **2 marks**

1   ....

    ....

2   ....

....

11 State an advantage and a disadvantage of demonstrations as a method of protest.   **2 marks**

    Advantage: ....

    ....

    ....

    Disadvantage: ....

    ....

    ....

Source B: Brexit

On 23 June 2016, a referendum was held throughout the UK on whether the UK should remain a member of the European Union (EU) on the new terms negotiated by the then Conservative Prime Minister, David Cameron. The public voted by 52 per cent to 48 per cent to leave the EU.

The UK ceased to be a member of the EU in January 2020, and there was a transition period of continued rights of membership until January 2021, unless an extension was requested in order to agree the terms of a new trade and other agreements with the EU.

12 Most Members of Parliament in 2016 wanted the UK to remain in the European Union. Examine why they did not just ignore the result of the referendum.

In your response you should refer to **Source B** and examples of other groups besides MPs who influenced the debate about Brexit. **8 marks**

....

....

....

....

....

....

....

....

....

....

....

Section D Active Citizenship: the Investigation

13 Explain how your choice of investigation relates to the citizenship specification. 　　2 marks

....

....

....

....

14 Discuss why you chose to work on your own or as a part of a group when undertaking your Investigation. 　　4 marks

....

....

....

....

....

15 Analyse the issues that can or did arise relating to undertaking research into your area of investigation. 　　6 marks

....

....

....

....

....

....

....

16 Justify your choice of investigation topic as being related to citizenship studies.

Your answer should refer to:

- the nature of the topic you investigated
- how this topic is a related to the specification
- why the topic is a citizenship issue
- how this topic helped you develop your citizenship skills and knowledge. 　　12 marks

....

....

....

Workbook answers at **www.hoddereducation.co.uk/workbookanswers**